The Poetry of John Galsworthy

John Galsworthy was born at Kingston Upon Thames in Surrey, England, on August 14th 1867 to a wealthy and well established family. His schooling was at Harrow and New College, Oxford before training as a barrister and being called to the bar in 1890. However, Law was not attractive to him and he travelled abroad becoming great friends with the novelist Joseph Conrad, then a first mate on a sailing ship.

In 1895 Galsworthy began an affair with Ada Nemesis Pearson Cooper, the wife of his cousin Major Arthur Galsworthy. The affair was kept a secret for 10 years till she at last divorced and they married on 23rd September 1905.

Galsworthy first published in 1897 with a collection of short stories entitled "The Four Winds". For the next 7 years he published these and all works under his pen name John Sinjohn. It was only upon the death of his father and the publication of "The Island Pharisees" in 1904 that he published as John Galsworthy.

His first play, The Silver Box in 1906 was a success and was followed by "The Man of Property" later that same year and was the first in the Forsyte trilogy. Whilst today he is far more well know as a Nobel Prize winning novelist then he was considered a playwright dealing with social issues and the class system. Here we publish Villa Rubein, a very fine story that captures Galsworthy's unique narrative and take on life of the time.

He is now far better known for his novels, particularly The Forsyte Saga, his trilogy about the eponymous family of the same name. These books, as with many of his other works, deal with social class, upper-middle class lives in particular. Although always sympathetic to his characters, he reveals their insular, snobbish, and somewhat greedy attitudes and suffocating moral codes. He is now viewed as one of the first from the Edwardian era to challenge some of the ideals of society depicted in the literature of Victorian England.

In his writings he campaigns for a variety of causes, including prison reform, women's rights, animal welfare, and the opposition of censorship as well as a recurring theme of an unhappy marriage from the women's side. During World War I he worked in a hospital in France as an orderly after being passed over for military service.

He was appointed to the Order of Merit in 1929, after earlier turning down a knighthood, and awarded the Nobel Prize in 1932 though he was too ill to attend.

John Galsworthy died from a brain tumour at his London home, Grove Lodge, Hampstead on January 31st 1933. In accordance with his will he was cremated at Woking with his ashes then being scattered over the South Downs from an aeroplane.

Index of Contents

COURAGE
TRUE DEEDS
LOVE (Two Versions)
BEAUTY
ACCEPTATION
SERENITY
DEDICATION
THE SEEDS OF LIGHT
DEVON AND OTHER SONGS FOR MUSIC
GAULZERY (GALSWORTHY) MOOR
LAND SONG OF THE WEST COUNTRY
VILLAGE SLEEP SONG
DEVON TO ME!
THE CLIFF CHURCH (WEMBURY)
COUNTING THE STARS
THE MOOR GRAVE
THE COVE
MOUNTAIN LOVERS
HIGHLAND SPRING
THE DOWNS
ON A SOLDIER's FUNERAL
OLD YEAR
WIND
STREET LAMPS
STRAW IN THE STREET
RHYME AFTER RAIN
LOVE'S FLOWER
ROSE AND YEW
MAGPIE
THE MOON AT DAWN
RHYME OF THE LAND AND SEA
FAST
THE GOLDEN GIPSY
MOUNTAIN AIR
TITTLE-TATTLE
THE FLOWER
VOICE IN THE NIGHT
AVOWAL
IN TIME OF WAR
VALLEY OF THE SHADOW
THE BELLS OF PEACE
PICARDY
YOUTH'S OWN
WONDER
UNKNOWN
THE PRAYER
I ASK!
TIME

REMINDER

Each star, to rise, and sink, and fade —
Each bird that sings its song and sleeps —
Each spark of spirit fire that leaps
Within me — of One Flame are made!

ERRANTRY

Come! Let us lay a lance in rest,
And tilt at windmills under a wild sky!
For who would live so petty and unblest
That dare not tilt at something ere he die,
Rather than, screened by safe majority,
Preserve his little life to little ends.
And never raise a rebel cry!

Ah! for a weapon so sublime,
That, lifted, counts no cost of woe or weal,
Since Fate demands it shivered every time!
When in the wilderness of our charge we reel
Men laugh indeed — the sweeter heavens smile,
For all the world of fat prosperity
Can not outweigh that broken steel!

The echo of out challenging
Sets swinging all the bells of ribaldry.
And yet those other hidden bells that ring
The faint and wondering chimes of sympathy
Within the true cathedral of our souls —
So, crystal-dear, the shepherd's pipe will move
His browsing flock to reverie

God save the pennon, in the morn,
That signals moon to stand, and sun to fly;
That flutters when the weak is overborne
To stem the tide of fate and certainty.
It knows not reason, and it seeks no fame.
But has engraven round its stubborn wood:
"Knight-errant, to Eternity!"

So! Undismayed beneath the clouds
Shall float the banner of forlorn defence —
A jest to the complacency of crowds,
But haloed with the one diviner sense:
To hold itself as nothing to itself;
And in the quest of the imagined star
To lose all thought of recompense!

COURAGE

Courage is but a word, and yet, of words
The only sentinel of permanence,
The ruddy watch-fire of cold winter days.
We steal its comfort, lift our weary swords.
And on For faith — without it — has no sense.
And love to wind of doubt and tremor sways,
And life for ever quaking marsh must tread

Laws give it not, before it prayer will blush,
Hope has it not, nor pride of being true,
'Tis the mysterious soul which never yields,
But hales us on and on to breast the rush
Of all the fortunes we shall happen thro',
And when Death calls across his shado'wy fields—
Dying, It answers "Here! I am not dead!"

TRUE DEEDS

There is a Lantern of true, silent deeds
Swinging refulgent in the spacious air.
Where restless words, those misty messengers
Sob out their subtle hearts with yea and nay.
And, like to myriad insects fluttering.
Brush with their wings that spiring crystal horn
That keeps inviolate a constant light.

'Tis the presiding sun at every birth.
The soft consoling moon at every death;
And in the middle watches of our life
What is it but the one sweet single star,
Whose twinkle, like the laughter of dear thoughts.
Upon the feeble vadings of our hearts
Sheds ever rays of tender irony!

Come night, come day, it knows no faltering.
Swung o'er the hubbub of a windy world.
No victory, but it doth halo round.
No sad defeat, whose wounds it hath not bathed;
And in those trackless wilds where nothing's done —
A mournful eye, its faint far glimmering
Peers through the distance everlastingly.

LOVE

O Love!—that love which comes so stealthily,
And takes us up, and twists us as it will—
What feverer'd hours of agony 'twill bring!
How oft we wake and cry "God set me free
Of Jove — to never love again!" And still
We fall, and clutch it by the knees, and cling
And press out lips — and so, once more arc glad!

And if It go, or if it never come,
Through what a grieving wilderness of pain
We travel on! In prisons stripped of light
We blindly grope, and wander without home
The friendless winds that sweep across the plain—
The beggars meeting us at silent night—
Than we, are not more desolate and sad!

LOVE (Earlier version)

Like lights that pass, each motion of the mind
Flies through the world, seeking its fellow thought;
And if but in the twinkling of his days
A man shall chance to meet the kindred one —
Then happiness! No more he needs to bum
Beside the fire of dearth that pipe, whose smoke
Prays to the heedless stars of lonely men.

Then in a rare and wonderful abode.
Where wit comes not, and thinking has no part,
A tender comedy is played and played.
That holds the magic meaning of the spheres.
And than the murmur of two meeting rills
Has no more sense — yet — all the sense there is
In this, our dream, and that, our coming sleep.

And when it's gone, or if it never come.
Then in the grieving dark we grope along;
Within the shuttered mazes of our souls
We wander, and again fall wandering.
The endless winds that sweep across the plain.
Beggars who meet us in the silent night.
Are not more shorn of company than we!

BEAUTY

Beauty is not a set and flawless rule;
She spells the mist, and with a silver wing
Hovers upon the shades of grey and brown
No less than on a rich embroidery
She IS a kind of rhythm, an accord
Of dreaming notes, so vague and mystical
That on a breath irrelevant they fade.

She subtly whispers her imaginings,
And hath a tender breath mote delicate
Than far blown scent of gone on distant hills
If we but catch the glimmer of her wing,
The witchery! We needs must follow her!
If never on our path she comes along—
Then are we lost, for always we are blind

The phantasy of yearning and of hope.
She comes to naught in Comprehension's grasp.
No feather balanced on the Southern gale
Is more impalpable than Beauty's face
We shall pursue her till out days are out.
If e'er she vanish. Life is spent — 'tis time
To draw the curtain for a last goodnight!

ACCEPTATION

Blue sky, grey stones, and the far sea.
The lark's song trilling over me;
Grey stones, blue sky, and the green weed —
You have no sense that I can read;
Nor on the wind's breath passing by
Comes any meaning melody!
Blue sky, grey stones, and the far sea.

Lark's song, green weed, wind melody —
You are! And must accepted be!

SERENITY

The smiling sea
And dunes and sky
Dream, and the bee
Goes dreaming by.

In heaven's field
Moon's scimitar
Is drawn to shield
One dreaming star

The dreaming flowers
And lovers nod
Serene these hours—
Serene is God

DEDICATION

Thine is the solitude that rare flowers know,
Whose beauty holds the charm of secrecy;
Of all the flowers that in the garden grow,
None other has thy sweet supremacy.
For thine's the oldest secret in the world:
How to be loved, and still to keep apart —
Flower full blown, and bud not yet unfurled —
Gold-fortuned I, whose very breath thou art!

THE SEEDS OF LIGHT

Once of a mazy afternoon, beside that summer sea,
I watched a shoal of sunny beams come swimming close to me
Each was a whited candle flamelet, flickering in air.
Each was a silver daffodil astonied to be there,
Each -was a diving summer star, its brightness come to lave,
And each a little naked spirit leaping on the wave

And while I sat, and while I dreamed, beside that summer sea.
There came the fairest thought of all that et came to me.

The tiny lives of tiny men, no more they seemed to mean
Than one of those sweet seeds of light sown on that water green.
No more they seemed, no less they seemed, than shimmerings of sky—
The little sunny smiles of God that glisten forth and die

DEVON OTHER SONGS FOR MUSIC

GAULZERY (GALSWORTHY) MOOR

Moor of my name, where the road leads high.
Thro' heather and bracken, gorse and grass.
Up to the crown of the western sky,
A questing traveller, slow, I pass.
Silent and lonely the darkening moor.
The beasts are bedded, the birds are gone.
Never a farm, nor a cottage door,
And I on the road alone — alone;
And the south-west wind is beginning to croon,
And a listening lonely pine-tree sways;
And behind it is hanging a golden moon
For a resting sign at the cornerways.
A thousand years since the stranger came.
And homed him here, and gave me name.

LAND SONG OF THE WEST COUNTRY

The lanes are long, and 'ome is for.
But we'll go joggin', joggin' on
Up dimsy sky, 'ere comes a star,
Over the bank the flowers peep
To see if 'us the time to sleep.
But we'll go joggin' on

The sunset's sinkin' down apace.
But we'll go joggin', joggin' on
The land's all like a maiden's face,
The more yu look the Jess yu see,
'Tis all a movin' mystery,
And we'll go joggin' on

The trout are risin' m the stream.
We ford it, joggin', joggin' on
The mill-wheel's turnin' in a dream,
The chafer's boomin' over'ead,

And every lidd'l bird's m bed.
And we go joggin' on

The cottages are prayin' smoke.
As -we go joggin', joggin' on.
The 'ayrick's bonneted a-poke;
The beasts are chewin' at their ease
The evenin' cud beneath the trees.
As we go joggin' on.

There's many a teasin' drop o' rain
As we go joggin', joggin' on.
And many a brave while fine again.
There's many a dip and many a rise.
And many a smile o' dinky eyes.
There's many a scent, and many a tune.
And over all the lidd'l mune
As we go joggin' on.

VILLAGE SLEEP SONG

Sleep! all who toil.
No longer creaks the harvest wain,
For sleeping lies the harvest day,
Asleep the winding leafy lane
Where none's afoot to miss his way

Sleep! village street,
You've stared too long upon the sun,
Now turn on to the gentle moon
Sleep, windows! for your work is done.
Tomorrow's light will come too soon!

Sleep! Sleep! the heat
Is over in the darkened home
A night-jar's spinning in the brake.
And — hark! — the floating owls have come
To try and keep the hours awake

Sleep! honey hives!
And swallow's flight, and thrushes' call!
Sleep, tongues, a little, while you may,
And let night's cool oblivion fall
On all the gossip of the day

Sleep! men and wives,

A sweetness of refreshment steal;
The morning star can vigil keep;
Too quickly turns the slumber wheel!
And all you little children, sleep!

DEVON TO ME!

Where my Cithers stood
Watching the sea.
Gale-spent herring boats
Hugging the lea,
There my Mother lives.
Moorland and tree
Sight o' the blossom!
Devon to me!

Where my fathers walked.
Driving the plough.
Whistled their hearts out—
Who whistles now?
There my Mother bums
Fire-faggots free
Scent o' the wood-smoke!
Devon to me!

Where my fathers sleep,
Turning to dust.
This old body throw
When die I must!
There my Mother calls.
Wakeful is She!
Sound o' the 'west-wind!
Devon to me!

Where my fathers lie.
When I am gone.
Who need pity me
Dead? Never one!
There my Mother clasps
Me. Let me be!
Feel o' the red earth!
Devon to me!

THE CLIFF CHURCH (WEMBURY)

Here Stand I,
Buttressed over the seal
Time and sky
Take no toll from me

To me, grey—
Wind grey, flung with foam—
Ye that stray
Wild-foot, come ye home!

Mother, I—
Mother I will be!
Ere ye die,
Heat! O sons at seal

Shall I fall—
Leave my flock of graves?
Not for all
Your rebelling waves!

I stand fast —
Let the waters cry!
Here I last
To Eternity!

COUNTING THE STARS

The cuckoo bird has long been dumb,
And owls instead and flitting jars
Call out, call out for us to come,
My Love and me, to count the stars;
And into this wide orchard rove —
The whispering trees scarce give us room.
They drop their petals on my Love
And me beneath the apple bloom.

And each pale petal is alive
With dew of twilight from the sky,
Where all the stars hang in their hive —
Such scores to count, my Love and I!
The boughs below, the boughs above.
We scatter, lest their twisted gloom
Should stay the counting of my Love
And me, beneath the apple bloom.

And when the Mother Moon comes by
And puts the little stars to bed.
We count, my timid Love and I,
The pretty apple stars instead;
Until at last all lights remove.
And dark sleep, dropping on the combe,
Fastens the eyelids of my Love
And me beneath the apple bloom

THE MOOR GRAVE

I lie out here under a heather sod,
A moor-stone at my head, the moor-winds play above.
I lie out here. ... In graveyards of their God
They would not bury desperate me who died for love!

I lie out here under the sun and moon;
' Across me bearded ponies stride, the curlews cry.
I have no little tombstone screed, no; "Soon
To glory shall she rise!" — but deathless peace have I!

THE COVE

Here the waves a refuge find,
Hunted ram, and sobbing wind.
And darling sun
To the velvet-thatchèd homes
Soft the sea-song silence comes
When day is done

Here's the safeguard of each hill,
And the telling of the oil
To Its dear sea
Home to rest, the south wind bongs
Ever drifted mutterings
Of tyranny

Ships, like drunken sailors, reel.
Ships, like silver shadows steal
Along the sky
Rocks arc green with wind-blown things.
Seaweeds furl their feathered rings.
And seabirds cry

Corner true! thou shyest gem,
Clinging to the jealous hem
Of weary earth!
Heart's delight shall never fail.
So thou keep thy hidden tale
Of grief and mirth!

MOUNTAIN LOVERS

The dawn's pale finger from her eye
Is brushing out the cobweb sleep,
See how the crimson clothes the sky,
And out of dark the mountains leap!
Now guides and hunters strap their gears.
The birds peep out, the mice run in,
A snow-wind moves the nose to tears,
As flowers to open just begin
When moon fades out with tilting horn,
And sleepy boys lead sleepy goats —
Then hand in hand with Lover Hope
The strong-eyed, with our feet a-swing
We'll go a-marching up the slope
Of Young Enchantment's promising

And now the dock is set at noon,
The butterflies ate kittens black;
And cowbells tumble out a tune
Which yellow bees do mumble back
We've climbed the snow into the sky,
Below, streams run a tinkling race.
And valleys glisten drowsily,
For all the world lies on its face.
The crystals bubble from the pine.
And grasses teem with little legs —
Then drink the cup of Lover Joy,
Who, silver-naked, goes about;
Till eager heart has got its cloy
Of wine that chases trouble out.

Now Sun has mellowed out the day.
And shadows play us hide and seek;
The cricket's legs have had their say.
And burned is every traveller's cheek.
Blueberries are ripe and warm.
Sparkle-fairies swim to land;
Hay is packing to the farm.

Cows, for milkmaids begging, stand.
Flaky trouts smoke in the dish.
Amber brews invite the throat —
Then let full plenty's droning song
Play harvest music to your ear:
Brave Lover Rest has come along
To drug the senses of his dear.

Dew is blessing all the air.
Steel-bright stars are winking points.
Hush is fallen, eyelids stare.
Rheum comes crackling at the joints
Woodsmoke tingles m the nose,
Moon goes dying like a sail,
Frost is nipping at the toes,
Drowsy drags the evening tale
Windy clouds like flighting geese,
Mountain-mad, the heavens haunt —
Then take the kiss of Lover Sleep,
Who slyly steals the light of eyes—
Let monk and maid, and martyr, keep
Their vigils, chant their threnodies!

HIGHLAND SPRING

There's mating madness in the air.
Passionate, grave! The blossoms burst.
The burns run quick to lips a-thirst;
And solemn gaze young maids, heart-free.

The white clouds race, the sun rays flare
And turn to gold the pallid mist;
With greedy mouth the Spring has kissed
The wind that links the sky with sea.

The blue and lonely mountains stare.
As if to draw the blue above.
The hour is come! O Flower of Love!
I can no longer keep from thee!

THE DOWNS

O Tire Downs high to the cool sky
And the feel of the sun-warmed moss!

And each cardoon, like a full moon
Fairy-spun of the thistle floss,
And the beech-grove, and a wood-dove,
And the trail where the shepherds pass,
And the lark's song, and the wind-song,
And the scent of the parching grass!

ON A SOLDIER'S FUNERAL

No pipes have skirled;
But heaven's wildest music blares;
Above the compound lightning flares.
The rain is whirled.

No drums shall roll —
Only a private soldier gone!
The cold light paints no funeral stone —
No bell need toll!

He lived his tame
And little day of silent tasks
And silent duty — no one asks
To know his name.

The milestones fade
Along the road that he has come.
No cheer of music takes him home —
His wage is paid.

The wind shrills high;
The darkened day is chasing grief
With lash of blinding rain — and brief
The footfalls die.

OLD YEAR

Tonight Old Year must die.
And join the vagabonding shades of time,
And haunt, and sob, and sigh
Around the tower where soon New Year will chime

How fast the slim feet move!
The fiddles whine, the reedy oboes toot.
Lips whisper, eyes look love —

And Old Year's dying, dying underfoot!

So mute and spent, so wan —
Poor corse—beneath the laughter flying by;
The revel dances on
And treads you to the dust— condemned to die!

The moonlight floods the grass.
The music's hushed, and all the festal dm.
The pale musicians pass.
Each clasping close his green-cased violin

Old Year! — not breathing now.
Along the polished floor you lie alone,
I bend, and touch your brow—
The dead year, that has slipped away and gone!

WIND

Wind, wind — heather gipsy.
Whistling in my tree!
All the heart of me is tipsy
On the sound of thee!
Sweet with scent of clover.
Salt with breath of sea.
Wind, wind — wayman lover.
Whistling in my tree!

STREET LAMPS

Lamps, lamps! lamps everywhere!
You wistful, gay, and burning eyes,
You stars low-driven from the skies
Down on the rainy air

You merchant eyes, that never tire
Of spying out our little ways.
Of summing up our little days
In ledgerings of fire—

Inscrutable your nightly glance,
Your lighting and your snuffing out,
Your flicker through the windy rout.
Guiding this mazy dance

O watchful, troubled gaze of gold.
Protecting us upon our beats —
You piteous glamour of the streets.
Youthless — and never old!

STRAW IN THE STREET

Straw in the street!
My heart, oh! hearken —
Fate thrums its song of sorrow!
The windows darken . . .
O God of all tomorrow!

Straw in the street!
To wintry sleeping
Turns all our summer laughter.
The brooms are sweeping . . .
There's naught for me hereafter!

RHYME AFTER RAIN

Starry-eyed is April morn,
Rainbells glitter on the thorn.
Birds are tuning down the lane
Patter song of fallen rain
Spring can grieve, but Spring can be
Very life of minstrelsy!
Gather the sob, gather the song!
Neither will last, neither will last!
All is yours, but not for long —
Life travels fast!

Rainbow's dipping out to sea.
Lambs are whispering devilry.
Leaves are sweet as e'er you've seen.
Sun is golden, grass is green.
Meadow's pied with flowers wet,
Thrushes sing "Forget, forget!"
Gather the grey, gather the gleam!
Neither will last, neither will last!
Certainty— 'tis but a dream!
Life travels fast!

Gorse has lit his lanterns all,
Cobwebbed thrift's a fairy ball.
Earth it smells as good as new.
Winds are merry, sky is blue.
Spring has laughter, Spring has tears,
Life has courage, life has fears.
Gather the tears, gather the mirth!
Neither will last, neither will last!
Old Year's death is Young Year's birth —
Life travels fast!

LET

My love lived there! And now
'Tis but a shell of brick,
New-painted, flowered about—
So far from being quick
As night when stats die out

From windows gaily wide,
Where once the curtained dark
My heaven used to hide.
The memories wan and stark
Troop down to me, outside!

LOVE'S A FLOWER

Love's a flower, 'tis born and broken.
Plucked apace, and bugged apart;
Evening comes, it clings — poor token —
Dead and dry, on lover's heart.

Love's the rhyme of a summer minute
Woven close like hum of flies;
Sob of wind, and meaning in it
Dies away, as summer dies.

Love's a shimmery morning bubble
Puffed all gay from pipe of noon;
Spun aloft on breath of trouble —
Bursts in air — is gone — too soon!

ROSE AND YEW

Love flew by! Young wedding day,
Peeping through her veil of dew.
Saw him, and her heart went fey —
His wings no shadows threw

Love flew by! Young day was gone,
Owls were hooting — Whoo-to-whoo!
Happy wedded lay alone,
Who'd vowed that love was true

Love flies by, and drops a rose—
Drops a rose, a sprig of yew!
Happy these— but ah! for those
Whose love has cried. Adieu!

MAGPIE

Magpie, lonely flying —
What do you bring to me?
Two for joy, and one for sorrow!
Loved to-day — is lost to-morrow!
Magpie! flying, flying —
What have you brought to me?

THE MOON AT DAWN

When, every dawn, the homeless breeze
Creeps back to wake the sleeping trees.
The moon steals down and no one sees

Yes! in the morn, no watcher there.
She turns a face, once angel fair.
And smiles as only wantons dare!

I saw her once, the insatiate moon,
Go stealing, coiffed in orange hood,
From Night, her lover, still in swoon—
All wicked she, who once was good!

RHYME OF THE LAND AND SEA

By the side of me, the immortal Pan,
Lies the sweetest thing of the sea;
In her gown of brine.
With her breast to mine.
And her drowned dark hair lies she!

But her smile — like the wine-red, shadowy sea.
When the day slides on and down —
By the gods, it is tender death to me!
In its waters dark I drown!
"O slave of mine! Thou mystery
Of smiling depths — I drown!"

PAST

The docks are chiming m my heart
A cobweb chime.
Old murmurings of days that die,
The sob of things a-drifting by
The docks ate chiming m my heart!

The stars have twinkled, and died out—
Fait candles blown!
The hot desires burn low, and gone
To ash the fire that flamed anon
The stats have twinkled, and died out!

Old journeys travel in my head!
They come and go —
Forgotten smiles of stranger friends.
Sweet weary miles, and sweeter ends
Old journeys travel in my head!

The leaves are dropping from my tree!
Dead leaves and flown.
The vine-leaf ghosts are round my brow,
For ever frosts and winter now
The leaves are dropping from my tree!

THE GOLDEN GIPSY

(from 'The Little Dream')

The windy hours through darkness fly —
Canst hear them, little heart?
New loves are born, and old loves die.
And kissing lips must part!
The dusky bees of passing years —
Canst see them, soul of mine.
From flower and flower supping tears
And pale sweet honey wine?

O flame that tread'st the marsh of time.
Flitting for ever low,
Where through the black enchanted slime
We, desperate, following go —
Untimely fire! we bid thee stay!
Into dark air above
The golden gipsy thins away . . .
So has it been with love!

MOUNTAIN AIR

Tell me of Progress if you will,
But give me sunshine on a hill —
The grey rocks spiring to the blue,
The scent of larches, pinks, and dew,
And summer sighing to the trees,
And snowy breath on every breeze
Take towns and all that you'll find there.
And leave me sun and mountain air!

TITTLE-TATTLE

Tittle-tattle! Scandal and japes.
Gibe, and gossip, and folly's rattle!
Ringed to fashion, caught like apes
In your cage of tittle-tattle!

Mean your skies.
And mean the ways you tread;
The meanness of your eyes
Is never fully fed.
You that have birth
In gold and grovellings!
You superfluity
Of miserable earth.

You trousered things
And women without souls —
Out of the sunlight
To your holes!

Tittle-tattle! Whisper and pry!
Sneers and snigger, and empty prattle!
Truth and Charity into a lie
To the tune of tittle-tattle!

THE FLOWER

There's a flower with a cup—
A cup of dew,
Golden god plucked it up
And gave it you

If you shake— let it spill —
Its pretty rain.
All the world will not fill
It up again

Careless death it must die,
And, like a weed.
In the sun ever lie
Disherited

VOICE IN THE NIGHT

(from 'To Let')

Voice in the night — crying —
Down in the old sleeping Spanish city.
Darkened under her white stars;

What says the voice — its clear lingering anguish?
Just the watchman telling his dateless tale of safety?
Just a roadman flinging to the moon his song?

No! 'Tis one deprived — a lover's prayer for pity.
Just his cry: "How long?"

AVOWAL

(from 'the Roof')

Thou art my Love, and I always,
That nothing rueful thee dismay.
My every waking thought intend
From this beginning to the end.
And m my sleep I dream of thee.
That unto me thou linkèd art.
And we arc sailing, thou and I,
To watch the silver fishes fly.
The stars uncounted m the sky.
And that great floorway of the sea
Then come with me if thou wouldst know
A summer that will never go.
Flowers unfading and the tune
Of sheepbells wandering in June
And I will conjure till these seem
Such part of elfin land to thee.
That backed on swallows thou shalt fly
And chase the thistle floating by.
And ride on moonbeams through the sky.
To rob dark night of ecstasy
I am a world devoted quite,
That lives but when thou'rt in my sight
Ah! Dwell in me, and I will try
To make thee happy till I die!

IN TIME OF WAR

VALLEY OF THE SHADOW

God, I am travelling out to death's sea,
I who exulted in sunshine and laughter.
Dreamed not of dying — death is such waste of me!—
Grant me one prayer; Doom not the hereafter
Of mankind to war, as though I had died not —
I who, in battle, my comrade's arm linking.
Shouted and sang, life in my pulses hot
Throbbing and dancing! Let not my sinking
In dark be for naught, my death a vain thing!
God, let me know it the end of man's fever!
Make my last breath a bugle call, carrying
Peace o'er the valleys and cold hills for ever!

THE BELLS OF PEACE

Lilies are here, tall to the garden bed,
And on the moot are still the buds of May;
Roses are here — and, tolling for our dead
The Bells of Peace make summer holiday

And do they hear, who in their Springtime went
The young, the brave young, leaving all behind.
All of their fate, love, laughter, and content.
The village sweetness, and the Western wind,

Leaving the quiet trees and the cattle red,
The southern soft mist over granite tor—
Whispered from home, by secret valour led
To face the horror that their souls abhor

Here m the starlight, to the owl's "To-whoo!"
They wandered once, they wander still, maybe.
Dreaming of home, dinging the long night thro'
To sound and sight fastened in memory

Here in the sunlight and the bracken green —
Wild happy roses starring every lane —
Eager to reach the good that might have been.
They were at peace. Are they at peace again?

Bells of remembrance, on this summer's eve
Of our relief. Peace and Goodwill ring in!
Ring out the Past, and let not Hate bereave
Our dreaming Dead of all they died to win!

PICARDY

When the trees blossom again.
When our spirits lighten—
When in quick sun and rain
Once more the green fields brighten,
Each golden flower those fields among,
The hum of thrifting bee.
Will be the risen flower and song
Of Youth's mortality

When the birds flatter their wings,

When our scars ate healing—
When the furry-footed things
At night again are stealing;
When through the wheat each rippling wave,
The fragrance of flower breath
Will bring a message from the grave,
A whispering from death

When the sweet waters can flow.
When the world's forgetting —
When once more the cattle low
At golden calm sun-setting;

Each peaceful evening's murmur, then.
And sigh the waters give.
Will tell immortal tale of men
Who died that we might live.

YOUTH'S OWN

Out of the fields I see them pass,
Youth's own battalion—
Like moonlight ghosting over grass,
To dark oblivion

They have a wintry march to go —
Bugle and fife and drum!
With music softer than the snow-
Fall, flurrying, they come!

They have a solemn tryst to keep
Out on the starry heath.
To fling them down, and sleep and sleep
Beyond Reveille — Death!

Since Youth has vanished &om our eyes.
Who of us glad can be?
Who will be grieving, when he dies
And leaves this Calvary?

WONDER

If God is thrilled by a battle cry.
If He can bless the moaning fight.

If, when the trampling charge goes by
God Himself is the leading knight;
If God laughs when the guns thunder,
If He yells when the bullet sings —
Then, bewildered, I but wonder
The God of Love can love such things!

The white gulls wheeling over the plough.
The sun, the reddening trees —
We, being enemies, I and thou —
There is no meaning in these.
There is no flight on the wings of Spring,
No scent in the summer rose.
The roundelays that the blackbirds sing —
There is no meaning in those!

If you must kill me — why the lark.
The hawthorn bud, and the corn?
Why do the stars bedew the dark?
Why is the blossom born?
If I must kill you — why the kiss
Which made you? There is no why!
If It be true we were born for this —
Merciless God, good-bye!

UNKNOWN

You who had worked in perfect ways
To turn the wheel of nights and days.
Who coaxed to life each running rill
And froze the snow-crown on the hill.
The cold, the starry flocks who drove
And made the circling seasons move;
How came your jesting purpose, when
You fashioned monkeys into men?

You who invented peacock's dress —
You, Lord of cruel happiness! —
Who improvised all flight and song
And loved and killed the whole day long.
And filled with colour to the brim
The cup of your completed whim!
What set you frolicking when we
Were given power to feel and see?

Why not have kept the stellar plan

Quite soulless and absolved from man?
What heavy need to make this thing —
A monkey with an angel's wing;
A murderous poor saint who reaps
His fields of death, and, seeing — weeps!
No! — if the saffron day could sigh
And sway unconscious — Why am I?

Unknown! You slept one afternoon.
And dreamed, and turned, and woke too soon!
The sorrel glowed, and the bees hummed.
And Mother Nature's fingers strummed.
And dock of dandelion was blown.
And yew-trees cast their shadows down,
Such beauty seemed to you forlorn—
And lo' — thus playboy, Man, was born!

THE PRAYER

If on a Spring night I went by
And God were standing there,
What is the prayer that I would cry
To Him? This is the prayer:

O Lord of Courage grave,
O Master of this night of Spring!
Make firm in me a heart too brave
To ask Thee anything!

I ASK

My happy lime is gold with flowers,
From noon to noon the breezes blow
Their love pipes, and the wild bees beat
Their drums, and sack the blossom bowers
Yet, stifling m the valley heat,
A woman's dying there below!

Between the blowing rose so red
And honey-saffroned lily-cup,
Receiving heaven, so I lie
But down the field a calf lies dead.
At this some burning summer sky
Its velvet darkened eye looks up

Behind the fairest masks of life
Dwells ever that pale constant death
Philosophers! What shall we say?
Must we keep wistful death to wife?
Or hide her image quite away.
And, wanton, draw forgetful breath?

TIME

Beneath this vast serene of sky
Where worlds are but as mica dust.
From age to age the wind goes by;
Unnumbered summer bums the grass.
On granite rocks, at rest from strife.
The æons lie in lichen rust.
Then what is man's so brittle life? —
The humming of the bees that pass!

FRIVOLS

MR. COLUMMY

Mr. Colummy is out in his park,
He and his tummy,
Mr. Colummy.
As soon as they see him the little dogs bark;
Oh! ever so rummy
Is Mr. Colummy.

Mr. Colummy has riz' with the lark;
Beginnings were slummy
With Mr. Colummy.
He once was a minnow, and now he's a shark.
He used to say: "Lummel"
Did Mr. Colummy.

Mrs. Colummy is pretty and dark;
Awfully plummy
Is Mrs. Colummy!
Her parents belonged to the island of Sark.
She's not very chummy
With Mr. Colummy.

Master Colummy — his cares do not cark!
That fat little dummy
Takes after his mummy;
There's never quite anything up to his mark.
Life's almost too crummy
For Master Colummy!

HOLIDAY SONG

Here's a day of cap and bells!
Cows shake out a silver dinning;
Shed your virtues, come a-sinning.
Leave your morals to their cells!

Birds are piping, insects hum;
Take the path of play and laughter!
Why go caring what comes after?
Nature's drum-sticks all a-drum!

Clowns and Christians count the loss!
Ope your mouth — let berries tumble!
Eat no more of pie that's humble!
Let your heart play pitch and toss!

When the cup of joy grows stale
Bunnies all shall cease their funning.
Sunflowers have enough of sunning.
Cats look tired, and kittens pale!

UNICORNS

If I were asked to take my pick
Of all the creatures fantastic.
Gryphons and Phoenixes and such,
Dragons and dolphins, and the much
Reported serpent of the sea.
Vampires, whichever they may be,
March hates, mad rabbits, or the Sphynx,
Or all the many missing links—

Well!
There's something to be said for fauns—
But I should choose white unicorns!

LINES WRITTEN IN THE AUTHOR'S COPY OF 'FROM THE FOUR WINDS'

SOLD FOR A CHARITY

I wrote this book and certify
That she's been mine in days gone by.
In fact the slim and timid tome
Has only known her parent's home.
There, with a slightly elder twin
She's stabled been, with kith and kin;
Thereof, lest any have a doubt
I write these words, and send her out.

DEDICATIONS TO TWO GODSONS

I

Small Friend, when your infatuate sire
Conferred on you the name of John,
And to myself expressed desire
That skyward I should lead you on,
How little did he know of me —
Of you, my godkin, even less!
But we conspirators must be
And bide up out unworthiness

Together we will tread the way
That leads to mansions m the sky,
Or, if We don't, at least we'll say
We surely mean to, by and by
And while we stay on solid earth
And still postpone our holy ends.
We'll, inch by inch, increase in girth.
And he, I hope, the best of friends

Small John, I fear when you grow up you'll say:
"They gave to me as pilot to the sky
A silly man who didn't know the way.
And couldn't put me wise — wonder why?
He never gave me book morocco-bound,
Or silver cup with christening date engraved;
He let me wander round and round and round.
And quite neglected for to get me saved!"

Well, little John, I freely do confess
That I'm no guide towards the better Land,
But, if in this, our earthly wilderness.
You falter, and should need a helping hand —
Then here it is, perhaps not over-clean.
And dabbled rather deep in ink and that—
But willing; and, at all events, I mean
You shall have nothing else to wonder at.

LINES WRITTEN IN A VOLUME OF 27 PLAYS BY JG

GIVEN AS A PRIZE BY THE 'SAVE THE CHILDREN' FUND

Who wins this prize has work cut out,
The volume is so very stout.
Indeed 'twill take many days
To read these twenty-seven plays

But then he/she need not take the thing
Au Sérieux, but have a fling,
Present the object to his/her Ma,
Or leave it in a motor car

June 8th, 1932

IN A VOLUME OF 27 PLAYS BY J. G.

SOLD ON BEHALF OF A HOSPITAL

The buyer gapes and stammers: "What!
You mean to tell me I have got
To read these Plays — to read them all!
Oh! no — the man's a criminal,
With twenty-seven mortal sins! —
Ye little fishes and your fins!
Too hot! It comforts me to think
They must have driven him to drink!"

Ah! yes, they did; and that is why
I make the buyer this reply:
"Far better burned than read, poor buyer,
So spare your eyes, and feed your fire!"

SOLD ON BEHALF OF A HOUSING SCHEME

STROPHE,
"An author who has what is called a vogue —
That can, like mushrooms, sprung up overnight —
A thing of air, and apt to vanish quite —
Runs every risk that be may seem a rogue
When signed editions he goes marketing.
Priced at as many guineas as he date.
And, trusting to the Public's want of flair.
Makes major money from a minor thing"

ANTISTROPHE
"But, carping Sir, your author is a bird
Who, like as not, believes that he will sing
And soar, until the booklet signed, will bring
A price that makes its present price absurd
A very peacock-fantail-phoenix, he;
The mote you warn him of his coming fall
Or tell him that he's nothing worth at all,
The more his pinnacle m air he'll see!"

FROM A WEARY WAYFARER

Lord! I plump for Princeton —
Peaceful there I be!
Peace and plump and Princeton
All begin with P!

O Friendly hat — hat of my friend!
And must I pack thee up and end
That brief encircling halo torn
From noble Masefield's peg, and worn
In ecstasy one hour Dear hat!
So much more beautiful than that
I left behind — from me depart!

Be crushed once more against his heart!

FOR LOVE OP BEASTS

PRAYER FOR GENTLENESS TO ALL CREATURES

To all the humble beasts there be.
To all the birds on land and sea.
Great Spirit! sweet protection give.
That free and happy they may live!

And to our hearts the rapture bring
Of love for every living thing;
Make of us all one kin, and bless
Our ways with Christ's own gentleness!

TO MY DOG

Mt dear! When I leave you
I always drop a bit of me—
A holy glove or sainted shoe—
Your wistful corse I leave it to.
For all your soul has followed me—
How could I have the stony heart
So to abandon you?

My dear! When you leave me
You drop no glove, no sainted shoe.
And yet you know what humans be —
Mere blocks of dull monstrosity!
My spirit cannot follow you,
When you're away, with all its heart
As yours can follow me

My dear! Since we must leave
(One sorry day) I you, you me,
I'll learn your wistful way to grieve,
Then through the ages we'll retrieve
Each other's scent and company;
And longing shall not pull my heart—
As now you pull my sleeve!

LOST!

In the grey wilderness — a dog!
Where are his friends — the scents he knew?
Who owned him, fed him, as he grew
From pup to shadow lost in fog?

His little world has thinned away;
He runs — a phantom; Fate will drive
Him up street, down street, all the day
And then at night no shelter give.

The trail is vapoured, gone the sense
Of human refuge; run and run,
'Tis all he can, not knowing where
Or whither — rum, and sniff, and shun!

In the grey wilderness — a ghost,
A thin, brown, helpless ghost astray!
Can no one stay him, show the way
To home, chase out that look: 'I'm lost!'?

DONKEYS

(from 'The Silver Spoon')

When to God's Fondouk the donkeys are taken —
Donkeys of Barbary, Sicily, Spain —
If peradventure the Deity waken
He shall not easily slumber again

Where in the street of the strata they have laid them.
Broken and dead of their burdens and sores.
He, for a change, shall remember He made them
(One of the best of His numerous chores).

Order from someone a sigh of repentance—
Donkeys of Syria, Araby, Greece —
Over the Fondouk distemper the sentence.
"For God's own forsaken— the Stable of Peace!"

NEVER GET OUT!

I knew a little Serval cat —

Never get out!
Would pad all day from this to that —
Never get out!
From bar to bar she'd turn and turn.
And in her eyes a fire would burn —
(From her zoology we learn!)
Never get out!

But if by hap a ray of sun
Came shining in her cage, she'd run
And sit upon her haunches where
Into the open she could stare.
And with the free that sunlight share —
Never get out!

That catling's jungle heart forlorn
Will die as wild as it was born . . .
If I could cage the human race
Awhile like her, in prisoned space.
And teach them what it is to face —
Never get out! . . .

PITIFUL

When God made man to live his hour,
And hitch his wagon to a star,
He made a being without power
To sec His creatures as they are
He made a masterpiece of will,
Superb above the mortal lot.
Invincible by any ill —
Imagination He forgot!

This man of God, with every wish
To earn the joy of Kingdom Come,
Will prison up the golden fish
In bowls no bigger than a drum
And though he'll wither from remorse
When he refuses Duty's call.
He'll cut the tail off every horse
And carve each helpless animal

No spur to humour doth he want,
In wit the earth he overlords.
Yet drives the hapless elephant
To clown and tumble on "the boards"

This man, of every learning chief.
So wise that he can read the skies.
Can fail to read the wordless grief
That haunts a prisoned monkey's eyes

He'll preach of "Mercy to the weak,"
And strive to lengthen human breath.
But starve the little gaping beak.
And hunt the timid hare to death.
Though, with a spirit wild as wind,
The world at liberty he'd see.
He cannot any reason find
To set the tameless tiger free.

Such healing victories he wins.
And drugs away the mother's pangs.
But sets his god-forsaken 'gins'
To mangle rabbits with their fangs.
Devote, he'd travel all the roads
To track and vanquish all the pains.
And yet— the wagon overloads.
The watch-dog to his barrel chains.

He'll soar the heavens in his flight,
To measure Nature's majesty;
Yet take his children to delight
In captive eagles' tragedy
This man, in knowledge absolute,
Who right, and love, and honour woos,
Yet keeps the pitiful poor brute
To mope and languish m his Zoos

You creatures wild, of field and air.
Keep far from men, where'er they go'
God set no speculation there —
Alack! We know not what we do!

AKIN

Who that has marked the white owl's flight
Or blessed the lark at noon.
Or listened of a summer night
And startled at the loon;
Who that has browsed with blunt-nosed sheep,
Or spied an adder drink.
Or seen a baby skunk asleep.

Or heard the bob-o-link —

Who so has fared, and felt no free
Delight within him run;
Then of the great freemasonry
Be sure he is not one.
But if his sentient ardour flow
For things that pad or fly.
With you and me — oh! surely know
He hath affinity.

America and England breed
Those who are brothers still,
For that the beasts they love, and heed
Bird music on the hill!

IMPRESSIONS

SILVER POINT

Sharp against a sky of grey.
Pigeon's nest in naked tree;
Every silver twig up-curled.
Not a budding leaf unfurled.
Not a breath to fan the day!

World aspiring and severe,
Not a hum of fly or bee.
Not a song, and not a cry.
Not a perfume stealing by —
Stillest moment of the year!

BOTTICELLI'S 'THE BIRTH OF VENUS'

The Spring fans her hair.
And after her fly little -waves,
Her feet are shod in pearly shoen,
And down her foam-white breast do shine
Petals encarnadine

Her eyes are deaths to care,
Her eyes of love ate tender caves
The blossoms blowing on the trees —
The leafy Spring's enchanted stir—

The humming of the golden bees —
Are but the voice of her!

BOTTICELLI'S 'PRIMAVERA'

Handmaids o£ the Queen of Level
Earth grows white with stars;
Young Fertility is leaping,
Soft the springing grasses teem;
Slothful days have left their sleeping —
You alone do dream!

Maidens of the Queen of Flowers!
Trees hang orange lamps;
All the winds are pollen blowing;
Through the failing golden light
Gentle Gravity is going —
Passion is the Night!

Maidens of the silver feet!
Violent Spring's awake!
Hearts are seeking, birds are nesting;
Earth below and skies above
Teach the hour of sweet unresting: —
All the world is Love!

THE CUP

Here is my Cup,
A crystal well,
Where the wind's rough fluting dies
To the thin-tuned sigh of a shell
The very breath
Of melody,
In sob and song
She's singing me!

Here is my Cup,
A fairy soul,
With the sun all gold on her curves,
And the moon milk-white in her bowl!
As twilight dark.
Like dew a-shine.
The goblet she

Of ev'ry wind

AUTUMN BY THE SEA

We'll heal the uncompanioned murmur of the swell.
And touch the drift-wood, delicately grey,
And with our quickened senses smell
The sea-flowers all the day.

We'll count the white gulls pasturing on meadows brown.
And gaze into the arches of the blue.
Till evening's ice comes stealing down
From those far fields of dew.

Now slow the crimson sun-god swathes his eye, and sails
To sleep in his innumerable cloak;
And gentle heat's gold pathway fails
In autumn's opal smoke;

Then long we'll watch the journey of the soft half-moon —
A gold-bright moth slow-spinning up the sky;
And know the dark flight — all too soon —
Of land-birds wheeling by.

Through all the black wide night of stars out souls shall touch
The sky, m this long quietude of things.
And gam brief freedom from the clutch
Of life's encompassings.

PROMENADE

All sweet and startled gravity.
My Love comes walking from the Park;
Her eyes are full of what they've seen —
The little hushes puffing green.
The candles pale that light the chestnut-trees.

The tulip and the jonquil spies;
The sunshine and the sudden dark;
The dance of buds; and Madam Dove,
Sir Blackbird fluting to his Love —
These little loves my Love has in her eyes.

In dainty shoes and subtle hose
My Love comes walking from the Park;
She is, I swear, the sweetest thing
That ever left the heart of Spring
To tell the secret: Whence the pollen blows!

THE FRANCE FLOWER

I stroll forth this flowerery day
Of "print-frocks" and buds of may.
And speedwells of tender blue
Whom no sky can match for hue

I love well my English home.
Yet far thoughts do stealing come
To throng me like honey-bees,
Till far flowers my fancy sees —

'Tis almond against the snows.
And gentian, and mountain rose,
And Iris, in purple bright —
The France flower, the flower of light!

SWEET OATH IN MALLORCA

If you had, suddenly, been where I've been.
Under the sun among the almond flowers,
If you had dreamed and seen what I have seen —
The old grey olives and the old grey towers;
If, in bewilderment there had come to you
Over the hills, beneath the evening star.
The tinkling of the sheepbells, or the blue
Gleaming from where the happy wild flowers are;
If you'd been wafted to that fairy-land.
And in delight been lost and lost again.
And, walking with me, waved a friendly hand
To children smiling with the eyes of Spain;
And in full day beheld the young moon fly —
Then had you sworn the same sweet oath as I!

AT VALDEMOSA

(Mallorca, January 2nd, 1930)

Lemons and roses — guide-book said—
A courtyard, and a simple bed
Or two, for that romantic purl
And so It was, when I was there

In quarters that were so confined
You may have found that lady's mmd
A little trying, day by day.
And so you did — or so they say!

But with such wonders for jour sight,
Such scatter of the stars at night.
Such sunset light upon the hills,
What need you reek of little ills?

You had a prospect to the sea
That certainly appealed to me.
The garden trim, the valley fair,
The folded hills, the limpid air.

The almond, winter-blossoming,
The buds not waiting for the Spring,
The olive trees, the tinkling bells
Of sheep among the asphodels.

What with the Paradise down there,
The scent of lemons on the air.
And all the music that you scored —
Chopin! I know you were not bored!

NOVEMBER

Leaves from the elm-trees flying—
Summer to autumn flown —
Out on the lawn is lying
Mulberry's golden gown

Never a bird is singing.
Never a plant has bloom,
Only the fantails winging
White on the windy gloom

We can no more remember
Perfume of rose or hay;

Far from this dark November
Beauty has passed away

Not till the Spring recapture
Joy as It flits along,
Shall we regain the rapture
Either of scent or song!

MERLE

The sea and sky are grey —
As with the grief of those who've mourned;
Yet through this drear December day
A lonely merle to song has turned.

Brave bird, for you no fears!
Though to the sun you're strange — as we.
Across the waste of these last years
Bereft of all hilarity.

Then, bird! be voice for all
The sad who have forgotten song.
Shake far that trilling lift and fall
Of notes, and take our hearts along!

DESERT SONG

As I came on from Santa Fe,
The desert road by night and day.
The desert wilds ran far and free
Beneath the wind of desert sea
But — ah! my heart! — to know again
The scent of rain, the scent of rain!

In fancy I would scale the air
Beyond those yellow mountains bare.
And so with dizzy bird survey
A thousand miles of shining day
And I would glean the gold of sun
And mark his curving glory run
Its fiery course, and, eager turn
My cheek and pallid brow to burn
But — oh! my heart! — to feel again
The wet of ram, the wet of rain!

And wakeful all the night I'd he
Watching the dark infinity,
Counting the stars that wheel and spin,
Drinking the frosty æther in.

And I would hear the desert song
That silence sings the whole night long,
And day by day the whisper pass
Of parching heat through desert grass.
But — Oh! my heart! — to hear again
The drip of rain, the drip of rain!

When I rode on from Santa Fe,
That desert road by night and day.
There came at last a little sigh,
A puff of white across the sky.
Then — ah! my heart! — knew again
The scent of rain, the scent of rain!

AT SUNSET

I've seen the moon, with lifted wing,
A white hawk — over a cypress tree;
The lover's star, the bloom of Spring,
And evening folded on Tennessee

I've seen the little streams run down —
All smoke-blue, lost in faerie,
And, far, the violet mountains crown
The darkness breathing on Tennessee

I've seen the beautiful, so dear —
And It has gone to the bean of me.
So there'll be magic ever neat
To me, remembering Tennessee

THE PASS OF THE SONG

Lone and far, lone and far
On a track that is strange and long.
From the morning's rim to the evening star
To the Pass of the Silent Song.

Far and lone, far and lone.
Where the rise and the rocks are bare.
And the sun has flamed, and the moon has shone
On the æons of desert air.

Lone and far, lone and far.
Till the eye to the summit wins,
And below, the plains and the mountains are,
And the lilt of the song begins.

Far and lone, far and lone
Will the tune of it lift and wend,
In a silent song of a world unknown
And a dream that will never end.

AUTUMN

When every leaf has different hue
And flames of birch trees blow,
And high against November blue
The white cloud's bent in bow.

When buzzard hawks wheel in the sun.
And bracken crowns the Cleave,
And autumn stains the heather dun,
And wan buds make believe,

When droning thresher hums its song
And tale of harvest proves,
And rusty steers the lane-ways throng,
And grey birds flit in droves.

Then bird, and beast, and every tree
And those few flowers that blow.
Against the winter hearten me
Who would no winter know!

DREAM HOUSE

Down on our house good shelter falls
From those high neighbouring white walls.
And here it dreams among the flowers
And bushes bright with summer showers.

Its creepered brick soaks up the smile
Of noon and afternoon, the while
The bees go tunnelling the deep
Dim lily bells that sway and sleep.

The day slips on, and sun's hot eye
Cools in the lime-trees, down the sky;
'Tis twilight now, the birds refrain
From song, and all is still again.

Now night creeps over, distance hides;
The white house — a tall iceberg — rides;
A chafer breaks the darkened swoon.
And white wide roses scan the moon.

FLOWERS

O my flowers! On your bosom
Sweet and pale the silver-cradled
Night shall swoon away with love

On your carpet gay, of blossom
Blue and gold, the softly-sandalled
Breeze shall dance from noon to noon

O my flower! At your coming
All the earth glows into gladness.
Dark and cloudy griefs remove

In my heart the wind is roaming
Wild, the grass is patched with sadness
Spring! my lovely Spring, come soon!

THE NATIVE STAR

I have sailed South to a new light.
New stars, and seen the Plough
Dip to the Cross, and watched the bright
Fish spraying from the prow.
Lagoons and palm groves I have spied.
And loom of mangrove tree;
Yet craved for a salt heaven wide
Above the English sea.

I have been far afoot among
Old deserts and great hills,
And trailed across the forests long
That feed the lumber mills.
At memory of smiling downs
Those grander visions pass,
For well I know to me the crown's
A day on English grass.

I have been mazed and mazed again
Where California glows.
And marvelled at a flowered Spain—
Her orange and her rose;
I've dreamed Japan, all cherry white,
Yet would I liefer see
The Springtime stars of blossom light
An English apple tree

In many countries I have stood
Where miracles have thronged
To God's imaginative mood.
And yet my heart has longed
For English sound and scent and scene
Though all my reason knows
They'll never be, have never been
Fit to compare with those

Why thus should be, I cannot tell,
Of Man it seems decreed
That he shall feel the moving spell
Of his especial breed
Muezzin call to night and room —
"Brothers, or near or far.
Be not dismayèd that each is born
Under his native star!"

TO LIBERTY

Bird, my bird, unwearied flying
Over the sands, over the sea —
Bird of Light, thou soul undying!
God that is not, yet shall be!

Bird, my bird, with eyes of morning.
Under the snow, under the night —
On! thou starry spirit, scorning

Refuge for thy wings of light!

Bird, my bird, the day is breaking
Over the sands, over the sea —
Rose beneath the darkness, waking
Summer's immortality!

Bird, my bird, I hear thee singing
Over the waste, over the foam.
Clear and high, the far white-winging
Song of Freedom, flighting home!

Bird, my bird, unwearied flying
Over the sands, over the sea —
Soul of Liberty, undying!
God that is not, yet shall be!

THE ENDLESS DREAM

PRAISED BE THE SUN!

If in a world where life is born of death.
And from the fate of dying none is free.
And the chief law is Strife, and every breath
Of man and beast and bird and fish and tree
Is daily drawn in dissolution's doubt —
If in a world like this there can be one
Among the rounding shows to single out
For praise — then will I praise the Sun!
The Sun, the Sun! — though it can deserts make,
And light its lanterns in their windswept bones;
I praise the Sun that doth with glory flake
The flowering meadows and the very stones;
That can the world transfigure to my eye.
And warm to substance all that shadows by.
Praising I live, and when I foundered be,
O thou beloved Sunlight, cover me!

TO BEAUTY

Beauty on your wings — flying the fat blue,
Flower of man's heart whom no God made,
Star, leaf-breath, and gliding shadow,
Fly with me too, awhile

Bung me knowledge
How the pansies are made, and the cuckoos' song!
And the little owls, grey in the evening, three on a gate.
The gold-cups a-field, the flight of the swallow;
The eyes of the cow who has calved,
The wind passing from ash-tice to ash-tree!

For thee shall I never cease aching?
Do the gnats ache that dance in the sun?
Do the flowers ache, or the bees rifling their gold?
Is it I only who ache?
Beauty! Fulfil me! Cool the heart of my desire!

SPRING

Come out! it's Spring!
The elm-trees! See! They're blossoming.
Ail crimson-painted! Here's a flower
Come open! Now with ev'ry hour
There'll be fresh pollen for that bee —
Oho! No longer sleepy he!

What song! What song
Those greening hedges breaks along!
God! There's performed in everything
A miracle of throat and wing,
Needs but a swallow to flit by
And print its pattern on the sky.

Oh! Smell this air!
The wind it wanders; everywhere
It plucks a scent. All! Exquisite
The ache of Spring that comes with it!
And whence it comes, or where it goes —
The troubling wind of Spring — who knows?

All now is still!
The sunlight's level on the hill
There goes a furry groundling Run!
You Spring-created rascal, run!
And — hark! The blackbird's evening shout:
"The Spring! The Spring! Come out! Come out!"

PEACE IN THE WORLD

(Message for the Livre d'or de la Paix, Geneva)

God send us wit to banish far
The incense and the reeking breath,
The lances and the fame of war.
And all the devilments of death.
Let there be wisdom and increase.
The harvest reconcilement brings.
So shall we see the eyes of Peace,
And feel the wafting of Her wings.

BURY HILL

To this green hill a something dream-like clings,
Where day by day the little blunt sheep graze.
Threading the tussocks and the toad-stool rings,
Nosing the barrows of the olden days
An air drifts here that's sweet of sea and grass.
And down the combe-side living colour glows,
Spring, Summer, Fall, the chasing seasons pass
To Winter, even lovelier than those

The dream is deep today, 'when all that's far
Of wandering water and of darkling wood.
Of weald and ghost-like Down combinèd are
In haze below this hill where God has stood.
Here I, too, stand until the light is gone.
And feed my wonder, while the sheep graze on!

SO MIGHT IT BE!

Death, when you come to me, tread with a footstep
Light as the moon's on the grasses asleep.
So that I know not the moment of darkness.
Know not the drag and the draw of the deep.

Death, when you come to me, let there be sunlight.
Dogs and dear creatures about me at play.
Flowers in the fields and the song of the blackbird —
Spring in the world when you fetch me away!

THE MOMENT WAITING

Folded is every sheep, the sunlight's gone,
A lonely bird re-takes its evening flight;
Warmth on the downs, and colour, there is none.
And yet a Presence — in this lingered light
Conjured of sky and the green-coated chalk.
Of air no longer sunlit, and so still—
Native and thin-embodied seems to walk.
As if devotional, upon this hill

I could be fancying the ghosts of all
Who vivified these heights m olden days
Lurk in the void, and wait for dusk to fall
And cover them on their remembered ways
There is a hushed suspense pervades this sweep
Of pallid grass, a spell unreal cast.
Even the fallen winds have feet that creep
Upon my sense, as if a spirit passed

'Tis in a moment waiting, such as now.
When all is wan, away to the far sea.
We of the life ephemeral can bow
In recognition of eternity
Sun and the moon and stars are sequestrate.
And time — it is not dawn nor noon nor night;
All is unbounded, and each mortal date
So little set as thistledown in flight.

MOON-NIGHT

The moon shines full, the elm-trees stand
Like sentinels, and shadows spill,
And up that quiet, unearthly land
The sheepbells with their tinkling fill
A silence reaching to the sky,
The rounded farm-stacks that were gold
Now moon-lit and unreal lie;
And all is magical and cold

But here, beneath my window, one
Magnolia flower blooms, alight.
Moon-glinted, lovely, and alone,
As fastened in the hair of night,
And from it to my nostrils creep
Such spicy odours as might move

To raptured waking all who sleep,
The very moon herself, to love

So may night breathe in beauty, when
My little flame blow s out, and I
Back to the fold return, foe then
It will be dream-like and goodbye
Will not be harder than it must;
For life will leave me with a kiss
Upon my brow of moonlit dust —
If night be beautiful like this!

AMBERLEY WILDBROOKS

Br this bright river bordering the mead
Beflagged by reed and rush and willow tree,
Where dragon-flies across the water lead
The wingèd rout of noonday revelry,
I stand ecstatic, silent, with a brain
Bemused, as stand bemused the tawny kine.
And heat high summer sink and lift again
And feel its spirit stealing into mine

Here when in winter-time the wild brooks brimmed
And with their salty flood annulled the earth.
Till with a lake the dreaming down was rimmed,
And wandering water-beauty came to birth,
With floating buds, and die green icy sky,
And far the sun so pale and pitying shone.
Here on this bank, no less bemused, stood I
Until the winter's mood and mine were one

Man is a dreamer, waking for a day.
Until the wild brooks of oblivion brim,
'Tis well his waking self should slip away.
And momentary dreaming comfort him,
For so he learns, before the long sleep comes.
That in himself revolves the starry scheme.
In him the winter's mute, the summer hums.
Just as it will be in the endless dream.

John Galsworthy – A Short Biography

John Galsworthy, eldest son of John Galsworthy (1817-1904), a solicitor and company director of Old Jewry, London, and Blanche Bailey (1835-1915), daughter of Charles Bartleet, a needlemaker in Redditch. His father's ancestors originated in Wembury, near Plymouth in England, and Galsworthy, for whom family origins were of significant importance, maintained a close connection with Devon. His more immediate family were considerably wealthy and well established in the shipping industry, and owned a fine estate in Kingston-upon-Thames called Parkfield, where Galsworthy was born on the 14th August 1867. At the age of nine he began education at Saugeen, a Bournemouth preparatory school, before starting at Harrow school in 1881 where he remained until 1886, distinguishing himself as an athlete.

His education at Harrow being successful enough to gain him entrance to Oxford, he began at New College to read law and gained a second-class degree with honours in 1889. Following Lincoln's Inn he was called to the bar in 1890. Despite this recognition he realised that he was not keen to actually begin practising law and so he resolved instead to look after the family's shipping business while specialising himself in Marine Law. This decision saw him take to the seas to destinations such as Vancouver, Island and South AFrica, though it was at the age of twenty-five on one particular journey to Australia, motivated by an (unfulfilled) intention to meet Robert Louis Stevenson on Samoa that he would being to realise fully his literary interests: though he was not considering becoming a writer at this time, his enjoyment of literature was enough to encourage an attempt at meeting a great writer and eventually enabled one of the most significant encounters of his life. He made the journey with his friend Edward Sanderson and, though he missed Stevenson, he met Joseph Conrad, a fellow future author famed for his novels which were often nautically themed. At the time Conrad was the first mate of the sailing-ship Torrens moored in the harbour of Adelaide, Australia; still very much focused on his ship-borne career, he was yet to begin his writing in earnest.

Indeed, though neither knew at the time, both Conrad and Galsworthy were at similar junctures in their lives, their time spent as sea acting as a transitional period during which each found their literary calling. It is perhaps owning to this unknown common ground that they became close friends. During his time on the Torrens Galsworthy recorded several details, offering a frank and valuable characterisation of Conrad while also illuminating his own experiences as a student of Marine Law.

"I supposed to be studying navigation for the Admiralty Bar, would every day work out the position of the ship with the captain. On one side of the saloon table we would sit and check our observations with those of Conrad, who from the other side of the table would look at us a little quizzically."

On his return to England and the cessation of his nautical voyaging, Galsworthy began an affair with the wife of his first cousin, Major Arthur John Galsworthy. Ada Nemesis Pearson Cooper (1864-1956), the daughter of Emanuel Copper, an obstetrician from Norwich, remained married to the Major for ten years and the affair remained secret for its duration. In order to conceal the affair they took considerable pains to avoid suspicion. One such tactic was to stay in a secluded farmhouse called Wingstone in the village on Manaton on Dartmoor, in Devon. In Galsworthy's decision to choose Devon as the location for their clandestine rendezvous we see evidence of Galsworthy's affection for the place of his father's origin. It was only when, in 1905, she divorced the Major that their affair became known following their marriage on 23rd September of that year.

Galsworthy now took to writing sometime after having met Conrad and his career began in earnest when, in 1897, his first work, From the Four Winds, a volume of short stories, was published under the pseudonym John Sinjohn. He succeeded this in 1898 with Jocelyn, his first novel, and then his second in

1900, Villa Rubein. In 1901 he published a second volume of short stories, A Man of Devon, which was the last of his work to be published under pseudonym. The first of his work to be published under his own name was The Island Pharisees in 1904, a novel of social observation, seasoned with flashes of satire and propaganda. His decision to write under his own name is arguably owing to the recent death of his father, either as a mark of respect to his name or because now he was able to publish freely without incurring the possibility of paternal disappointment at his choice of career. It also marked a shift in his professionalism; he had hitherto published with small, independent publishers, but The Island Pharisees was published by Heinemann, a far more established House and one with whom he remained for the duration of his writing career.

He arguably cemented his position and maturity as a writer when, in 1906, he saw the publication of both his first major play, The Silver Box, and the novel The Man of Property. Each was published to considerable critical acclaim, and to achieve both in such a short space of time was impressive. the Silver Box concerns the imbalance in the justice system with regards to criminals of differing class by contrasting the treatment of a poor thief and a rich thief, both of whom stole silver cigarette cases but for very different reasons. The complexity of individual experience when not dealt with in public is highlighted and questioned in a bravely critical manner; despite the clear issues it raises with class and privilege, the final night was attended by the Price and Princess of Wales. The Man of Property was the first novel in the famous The Forsyte Saga, a trilogy of novels with an 'interlude' between each one, written between 1906 and 1921. Dealing with the questions of status, class and materialism, The Man of Property introduces us to the Forsyte family, particularly Soames Forsyte, who is acutely aware of his status as 'new money' and equally keen to assert himself as a wealthy man. Jealous of his wife and desperate to own things in order to confirm his wealth to those observing him, he engineers a plan to keep his wife from her friends which backfires spectacularly when, instead of cutting her off, all Soames achieves is enabling her to have an affair. This drives Soames to terrible actions with terrible consequences, which Galsworthy depicts with confidence.

Very typically Edwardian, the novel focuses on conflict between property and art, and to a certain degree much of its emotional power is drawn from Galsworthy's own life, particularly his affair with Ada. Their rendezvous in the countryside of Devon mirror the manner in which Forsyte seeks to relocate his wife and; though theirs was a much healthier relationship, there are clear similarities. By examining the fragile nature of the class system and those moving within it Galsworthy offered an important perspective on the relationships between material wealth, personal happiness and obsession, and the manner in which these change over time. His contemporaries widely regarded the publication of this novel as marking the end of Victorianism. His friend Conrad praised it as "indubitably a piece of art" and, though the notoriously risqué D.H. Lawrence lamented the novel's timidity in the face of sexuality and sensuality, he considered it potentially "a very great novel, a very great satire".

Though he continued to write both plays and novels, it was his work as a playwright for which he was most celebrated by his contemporaries. Indeed, his next novel, The Country House, seems uncharacteristically unfocused, its satirical view of those belonging to the country set comparatively unremarkable and weakly characterised, while at times the tone of satire becomes one of ironic detachment. In 1909 he published Fraternity, an exploration of of the various connections between urban society and the social classes therein, though its representation of lower-class Londoners is utterly unconvincing and ill-informed. Remaining with the subject of the landed gentry and the society surrounding it, in 1915 he published The Freelands, which does not stray far from conservative discussions of capitalism, the rural economy and their interrelationship.

His drama, however, featured a convincingly muted realism, directed at a relatively small, educated and politically-aware audience. His social agenda is prevalent here too, and is represented in a simple and static manner producing arresting instances of high drama. This talent for creating moments of captivating theatre is complimented by an instinctual sense of balance enabling his narratives to vacillate between their emotional high- and low-points, ultimately reaching conclusive equilibrium. This is particularly evident in one of his most popular plays, Strife, published in 1909 and examining the antagonists in a strike at a Cornish tin mine. In this, and in 1910's Justice, he approaches his subject with sympathy, irony and balance, which establishes a position of narrative authority while garnering the audiences trust that he is representing his characters and their motives justly. Justice condemns the use of solitary confinement in prisons, a reformist agenda which caught the liberality of his contemporary audiences along with the home secretary, Winston Churchill. Despite he was careful to disassociate himself with politics and professed himself apolitical, he and his work were nevertheless aligned with the views of the Liberal establishment. He spent much of the duration of the First World War working in a field hospital in France as an orderly having been passed over for military service.

Despite the popularity and brilliance of his work, it was only in 1920 that he had his first true commercial success with The Skin Game, a melodrama dealing with ethics, property and class. The play was adapted by Alfred Hitchcock in 1931. Galsworthy, meanwhile, had turned down a knighthood in 1918, considering his work not sufficient to be made a knight of the realm. He did, however, accept the Belgian Palmes d'Or in the following year. In 1920 he published the second novel in the Forsyte Saga, In Chancery, in which he resumes many of the themes of the first novel, focusing on the marital disharmony between Soames Forsyte and his wife. Katherine Mansfield considered it "a fascinating, brilliant book" in her review in The Atheneum. Then, in 1921, he was elected as the PEN International Literary Club's first president. The concluding novel to The Forsyte Saga, To Let was published in 1921 with a kind of peace being found between Forsyte and his now-ex wife, though he is left contemplating his losses and his greed. More ironic treatment of class confusions followed in Loyalties, bringing with it more popular success which lasted until 1926 and Escape, the last of his popular plays. Though he enjoyed popular success it was inconsistent and relatively small. His Collected Plays was published in 1929.

Over the course of time the appreciation of his work has gradually shifted from his plays to his novels, and particularly the detail and intricacy of his chronicle of English social difference, tension and pretension in The Forsyte Saga. Its success encouraged Galsworthy to revisit Soames Forsyte in a second trilogy, A Modern Comedy, which follows Soames's obsessive love of his daughter Fleur. In its three volumes, The White Monkey (1924), The Silver Spoon (1936) and Swan Song (1928) he examines the English commercial upper-middle class and its ideologies, its instinct to possess as its only way of distinguishing itself manifested in the poisonous materialism of Soames. Interestingly, this emergent social class which he so vehemently criticises is the very class from which he emerged. He witnessed first-hand its insularity, its chauvinism, its restrictive and oppressive morality, its stubborn imperialism and its materialism, and it is this experience which enables him to write so comfortably about it. Swan Song is widely considered among the best of Galsworthy's writing for the depth of its exploration of society and its heightened emotional subtlety. In 1929 he was appointed to the Order of Merit, despite having turned down a knighthood earlier. He spent his last years writing a third trilogy, End of the Chapter, beginning in 1931 with Maid in Waiting, Flowering Wilderness in 1932 and concluding with Over The River in 1933. These are significantly less coherent works and are indicative of his deteriorating health. Indeed, in 1932 he was awarded the Nobel Prize, though he was too ill to attend the ceremony.

Throughout the course of his career he received honorary degrees from the universities of St Andrews (1922), Manchester (1927), Dublin (1929), Cambridge (1930), Sheffield (1930), Oxford (1931), and Princeton (1931). In 1926 New College, Oxford, elected him as an honourary fellow. In photographs he is portrayed as handsome, fastidiously dressed and dignified. He was unusually compassionate and this saw him involved in several charitable and humane causes throughout the course of his life, including penal reforms, attacks on theatrical censorship and campaigning for animal rights. Though he spent the majority of the final seven years of his life at his home in Bury, West Sussex, it was at his home in Hampstead, London, that he died of a brain tumour on 31st January, 1933, six weeks after having been too ill to attend the ceremony in honour of his receiving the Nobel Prize. According to demands made in his will he was cremated and his ashes scattered over the South Downs from an aeroplane. Also in his will was his wish to leave cottages to several of his astonished tenants. He is memorialised in Highgate 'New' Cemetery and in the cloisters of New College, Oxford, where he was an honourary fellow.

John Galsworthy – A Concise Bibliography

From the Four Winds, 1897 (as John Sinjohn)
Jocelyn, 1898 (as John Sinjohn)
Villa Rubein, 1900 (as John Sinjohn)
A Man of Devon, 1901 (as John Sinjohn)
The Island Pharisees, 1904
The Silver Box, 1906 (his first play)
The Man of Property, 1906 – First book of The Forsyte Saga (1922)
The Country House, 1907
A Commentary, 1908
Fraternity, 1909
A Justification for the Censorship of Plays, 1909
Strife, 1909
Fraternity, 1909
Joy, 1909
Justice, 1910
A Motley, 1910
The Spirit of Punishment, 1910
Horses in Mines, 1910
The Patrician, 1911
The Little Dream, 1911
The Pigeon, 1912
The Eldest Son, 1912
Quality, 1912
Moods, Songs, and Doggerels, 1912
For Love of Beasts, 1912
The Inn of Tranquillity, 1912
The Dark Flower, 1913
The Fugitive, 1913
The Mob, 1914
The Freelands, 1915
The Little Man, 1915
A Bit o' Love, 1915

A Sheaf, 1916
The Apple Tree, 1916
The Foundations, 1917
Beyond, 1917
Five Tales, 1918
Indian Summer of a Forsyte, 1918 – First interlude of The Forsyte Saga
Saint's Progress, 1919
Addresses in America, 1912
In Chancery, 1920 – Second book of The Forsyte Saga
Awakening, 1920 – Second interlude of The Forsyte Saga
The Skin Game, 1920
To Let, 1921 – Third book of The Forsyte Saga
A Family Man, 1922
The Little Man, 1922
Loyalties, 1922
Windows, 1922
Captures, 1923
Abracadabra, 1924
The Forest, 1924
Old English, 1924
The White Monkey, 1924 – First book of A Modern Comedy
The Show, 1925
Escape, 1926
The Silver Spoon, 1926 – Second book of A Modern Comedy
Verses New and Old, 1926
Castles in Spain, 1927
A Silent Wooing, 1927 – First Interlude of A Modern Comedy
Passers By, 1927 – Second Interlude of A Modern Comedy
Swan Song, 1928 – Third book of A Modern Comedy
The Manaton Edition, 1923–26 (collection, 30 vols.)
Exiled, 1929
The Roof, 1929
On Forsyte 'Change, 1930
Two Essays on Conrad, 1930
Soames and the Flag, 1930
The Creation of Character in Literature, 1931 (The Romanes Lecture for 1931).
Maid in Waiting, 1931 – First book of End of the Chapter (1934)
Forty Poems, 1932
Flowering Wilderness, 1932 – Second book of End of the Chapter
Autobiographical Letters of Galsworthy: A Correspondence with Frank Harris, 1933
One More River (originally Over the River), 1933 – Third book of End of the Chapter
The Grove Edition, 1927–34 (collection, 27 Vols.)
Collected Poems, 1934
Punch and Go, 1935
The Life and Letters, 1935
The Winter Garden, 1935
Forsytes, Pendyces and Others, 1935
Selected Short Stories, 1935

Glimpses and Reflections, 1937